Following Native American Trails

A Trumpet Club Special Edition

Special Edition
Created by Angel Entertainment, Inc.

Library of Congress Cataloging-in-Publication Data

Grenier, Nicolas
   Following Native American Trails / Author, Nicolas Grenier; ill.,
   Donald Grant. Includes index. Translation of: Sur les traces des
   Indiens d'Amerique. Summary: Examines the everyday life of
   American Indians in a tribal community.
   1. Indians of North America — Social life and customs. —
   Juvenile literature. I. Grant, Donald, ill. II. Title
   III. Series: Young Discovery Library; 9
E98.S7G8513   1988
306'.08997 — dc 19

Written by Nicolas Grenier
Illustrated by Donald Grant

Specialist adviser:
Dr. Philippe Jacquin, Modern
History Dept. University of
Lyons; author of **History of**
the Indians of North America

First U.S. Publication 1988 by
Young Discovery Library
217 Main St. • Ossining, NY 10562

YOUNG DISCOVERY LIBRARY

Following
Native American
Trails

YOUNG DISCOVERY LIBRARY

The first people in America?

Can you and your friends walk Indian file? Have you Indian wrestled? Is your mom on the warpath? You've seen lots of tepees, headdresses and smoke signals in your picture books and at the movies. So you think you know all about Indians?

First of all, why are Indians called Indians if they live in America? Well, when Christopher Columbus landed in the New World in 1492, he thought he was in India — he named the people he saw Indians. And that's what they've been called ever since!

In prehistoric times, Indian hunters drove bison to a cliff where the animals panicked and jumped over the edge.

Plains Indians in the 19th century

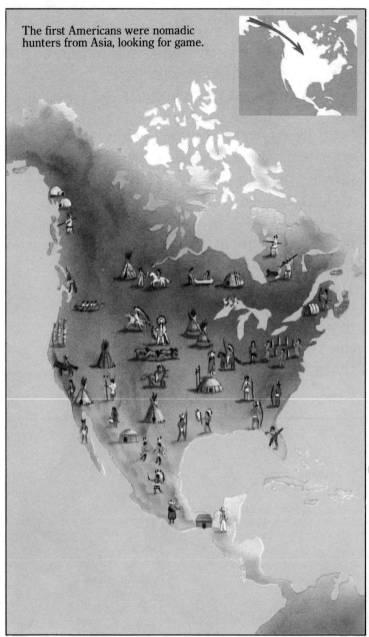

The first Americans were nomadic hunters from Asia, looking for game.

The Indians traveled far! If you look on a map or globe, you will see that the only thing that divides Asia from the uppermost part of North America is a narrow passage of water: the Bering Strait. Several times, the earth's climate got colder. This arm of the sea turned into a bridge of ice. That is how hunters from Asia reached the American continent thirty-five thousand years ago. Some stayed in the north and formed more than a thousand tribes, each with their own language. They made their homes on the plains, in the forests, in the mountains or deserts. Others went on to South America.

1. Cheyenne wearing ceremonial head-dress

2. Iroquois

3. Pawnee

The Indians worshipped the eagle and captured it for its feathers. The hunter hid, then the eagle came to eat the bait.

Pueblos, Navajos and Apaches lived in the Southwest, near Mexico, in a land of sun, canyons and deserts. By irrigating the arid soil, the Pueblos grew corn, tobacco and vegetables. They built adobe villages right on the cliffs, and entered their houses through the roof!

The hunter jumped up and caught it. He used the feathers to make a headdress.

Their arch enemies were the Apaches, who lived by hunting and looting. They were the first Indians to discover the horse, which was reintroduced by the Spanish long after it had disappeared from the continent in prehistoric times. The Navajos were skilled craftsmen who made baskets, blankets and jewelry.

The forests, rivers and Great Lakes of the Northeast were home to the **Hurons** and the **Iroquois.**

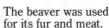

The beaver was used for its fur and meat.

The Indians had plentiful resources: they fished, dug clams, hunted the woods for game and cultivated the land to grow corn, beans, and squash. They also learned to survive harsh winters by wearing warm furs and snow-shoes so they

The Indians of Canada hunted moose.

could walk on top of the snow and hunt all winter long. They used the wood of the birch tree to make long houses, and its bark to make lightweight canoes. Tools and medicines were also made from the birch tree.

They caught and tamed bear cubs. The bear was one of their favorite animals.

Northwest Coast Indians

Along the Pacific coast,
the Indians lived off
the wealth of the sea:
mollusks, fish, seals,
walruses, sharks and
even whales, which the
Nootka and Makah hunted
aboard large dugout
canoes made from coastal
cedars.

What is a totem pole?

It is a tall pole of
carved, painted wood
decorated with the gods
and animals which
the clan worshipped.
The ceremonies of the
Northwest Coast
Indians took place
around these poles.

A totem used to protect a
house's occupants had a
hole cut in its base as a door.

Cheyenne, Arapaho, Kiowa, Sioux, Comanche and Blackfoot were tribes of the Great Plains between the Mississippi and the Rockies. Nomads and hunters, most of them followed the migration of the buffalos, on whom they depended for food and shelter. Not all Indians lived in tepees.

Each tribe had its own type of house: tents, huts of dirt or dried grasses. To make a tepee, the Indians stood twenty or so poles in a circle, then covered them with buffalo hides.

They left an opening at the top to let the smoke out. When it got too warm, they raised a few hides.

The Indians did not always have horses. Until the 18th century dogs were their beasts of burden.

The oldest means of transport, the travois.

Horses fascinated them. They were called 'sacred dogs' by the Comanches, and 'seven-dogs' by the Spanish.

Pictures and carvings honored horses who died in battle.

The horse became an indispensable companion for hunting, fighting, and transportation. The Indians caught, traded, and even stole them. The more they had, the richer they were. The Indians were very good riders. They could catch and tame a wild horse in one day.

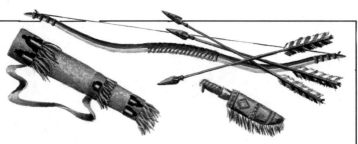

On the plains lived vast herds of
buffalo, large wild oxen weighing
almost a ton.
First, a dance was held to ask the
Great Spirit for a good hunt.
Then the hunters left on horseback,
armed with bows and spears. They
rode up close to the animals before
shooting their bows or throwing their
spears.

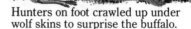

Hunters on foot crawled up under
wolf skins to surprise the buffalo.

All parts of the buffalo were used:
meat, fat, fur, skin, bones and horns.

Beaded moccasins

Buffalo meat was eaten fresh or dried

Tanning the hides

Turquoise
jewelry

Weaving a
blanket

The Native Americans were
skilled craftspeople, tanning hides,
drying meat, making tepees, weaving
blankets and decorating moccasins.

**In the village, the women did
the daily chores.**
They did the cooking and sewing.
They put up and took down the
tepees. A hunter could have
several wives in order to have
many children. Each birth was
a cause for rejoicing in the clan.

Little girls stayed at home where
they learned to help their mothers,
even while they played. Boys prac-
ticed riding and archery, waiting
for the day their fathers
would give them a pony
and take them hunting.

To purify his body, the Indian first sat in this 'sweat lodge', then bathed in a stream.

To be a hunter or warrior, it was not enough for a man to know how to ride a horse or use a bow and arrow: he had to be **initiated. For the Indians, religion was a part of everyday life.** Rocks, plants, animals and humans were all children of one Great Spirit. The Algonquins called it manitou. All living things were respected. Before cutting down a tree or killing an animal, the Indians asked the spirits for forgiveness. Teenagers had to know these rules before they could pass into adulthood.

Smoking the *peace pipe* as an offering to the spirits.

The shaman played an important role in the tribe. He had magic powers, acted as an intermediary between the spirits and humans, and cured the sick. He taught young boys to uderstand and respect nature. To become a shaman, an Indian first had to purify his body, then go off in the wild without food to wait for the spirits to visit him.
If he had a vision of an eagle, for example, he knew the bird would be his guardian spirit from that time on.

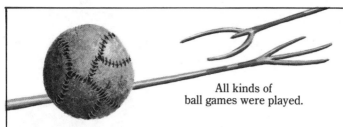

All kinds of
ball games were played.

The Indians' recreation
Even if their lives were hard and
food was scarce, the Indians still
enjoyed themselves at games.
One of the most well-known Indian
games is **lacrosse.**

In the game of knuckle-
bones, a needle had to be
threaded through little bones.

Several hundred
players, divided into two teams,
used rackets to try and send the
ball into the other team's goal.
One game could last all day.

Two players in
the hoop-and-
pole game.

The coming of the White Man

The French settled in Canada and Louisiana. The English came on the *Mayflower* to the East Coast. The Russians came by the Pacific, the Spanish from the south. What did all these White Men want? To trade, of course. The Indians were happy to trade furs for guns and liquor. But the White Man also wanted to take their land. The Indians would no longer rule over the land.

It all happened quickly. More
and more White Men arrived. They
needed more land. The Indians
trusted them and believed the
White Man's word and treaties.
But they soon had to defend their
land and their food: The White Man
was killing off the buffalo.

Little Big Horn. On June 25, 1876, Crazy Horse and Sitting Bull led a group of Sioux, Cheyennes and Arapahos into battle against the Americans. This was "Custer's Last Stand". But by the time victory came, the Indians were exhausted, starving, and divided.

On December 29, 1890, the massacre at **Wounded Knee** ended the Indians' resistance. Those who survived were forced onto reservations. One and a half million of their descendants still live on them.

Comanche. Move your hand like a snake.

Cheyenne. Pretend you are cutting your finger.

Indian. Rub your left hand twice.

Pawnee. Make a V with your index and middle fingers.

Crow. Rest your fist on your forehead.

Sioux. Pretend you are cutting your neck.

The Plains tribes all spoke different languages. To understand each other, they invented a sign language that even the White Man learned.

Sign language made it possible to indicate the names of tribes as well as animals and objects.

1. Greetings   2. How much   3. Beaver   4. Friend

Body movements often accompanied the sign language. To say "how much", the person turned sideways.

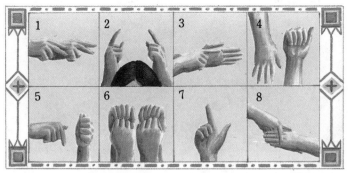

1. Dog   2. Buffalo   3. Cannot   4. Bad
5. Bow   6. Advice   7. Moon   8. Horse

The hands, body movements, and face painting all communicated messages.

Already killed an enemy.

War paint.

To make it rain for the corn.

After thunder and lightning comes rain.

1. Wounded an enemy
2. Killed with his fists
3. Discovered the enemy
4. Killed with a gunshot
5. Was wounded several times

Glossary

Buffalo: the name commonly used for bison, large wild oxen.

Manitou: Great Spirit for the Algonquins.

Mustang: wild horse.

Paleface: the Indians' name for a white man.

Papoose: baby.

Sachem: chief.

Shaman: religious leader, often called a "medicine man".

Squaw: woman.

Tomahawk: a stone hatchet with a wooden handle used by eastern tribes.

Wapiti: elk.

Index

Books of Discovery for children five through ten...

Young Discovery Library is an international undertaking — the series is now published in nine countries. It is the world's first pocket encyclopedia for children, 120 titles will be published.

Each title in the series is an education on the subject covered: a collaboration among the author, the illustrator, an advisory group of elementary school teachers and an academic specialist on the subject.

The goal is to respond to the endless curiousity of children, to fascinate and educate.